a simple plan

W9-CCD-841

a simple plan
GARY SOTO

CHRONICLE BOOKS
SAN FRANCISCO

YNF
811
SOT

Library of Congress Cataloging-in-Publication Data available.

ISBN-10: 0-8118-5828-6
ISBN-13: 978-0-8118-5828-1

Manufactured in the United States of America

Book Design: Michael Osborne Design
Cover Illustration: José Ortega

Distributed in Canada by Raincoast Books
9050 Shaughnessy Street
Vancouver, British Columbia V6P 6E5

10 9 8 7 6 5 4 3 2 1

Chronicle Books LLC
680 Second Street
San Francisco, California 94107

Acknowledgments—
Some of these poems appeared in the following magazines: *Askew, Cæsura, Crazy Horse, Green Mountains Review, Hubbub, Indiana Review, New Letters, Ploughshares,* and *Water-Stone Review.*

The author would like to thank Christopher Buckley and Carolyn Soto for the close readings of these poems.

THIS BOOK IS FOR CHRISTOPHER BUCKLEY

CONTENTS

PART ONE

WAITING AT THE CURB: LYNWOOD, CALIFORNIA, 1967
for Deborah Escobedo

When the porch light snaps on,
Moths come alive around its orange glow.
Mother pushes open the screen door and calls,
"*Viejo!* It's *Laugh-In*." Father is watering
His lawn, the one green he can count on. He can't count
On money, or his Dodgers slipping on the green
Rug of Chavez Ravine and into third place,
With nineteen games to go. "Be right there," Father says,
And then considers his daughter emerging in cutoffs
Cut too short. And what's with the gypsy blouse
And those 45 records on her thumb?
Maybe he could speak his mind about decency,
Maybe he could lift his hose and spray off this girl child
Who has gone too far. But he rolls the garden hose
Onto the sling of his arm. "Debbie, where you going
With no clothes on?" he asks. The daughter spins
The records on her thumb, and answers,
"Dad, this is how it is." She steps off the porch,
Cuts across the wet lawn, and waits at the curb
For a friend in her own cutoffs,
For the walk to the playground with two boys following.
She turns when the neighbor's screen door opens—
A woman in curlers yells to her own old man, "It's *Laugh-In*."
America is getting ready,
America is shoveling ice cream into Tupperware bowls,
America is setting up trays in front of snowy TVs.
This daughter wags a shaggy head of hair at the old folks,
Pulls at her cutoffs creeping up. *I gotta get outta here,*
She thinks, and spins the music of Motor City
On what will soon be a hitchhiker's thumb.

MOVIES & SHOES

Dead these many years,
You walk into my sleep.
What is it, Ernesto, thirteen years
Of stars scratching the sky
To get to us? Thirteen years
Of movies for me,
And for you, fan of
Cantinflas and Woody Allen,
A black screen? In
Mexico, you watched movies
Splashed onto bed sheets.
If an unlikely wind rippled the cloth
And pleated the face of Lola Alvarez,
Pouty beauty in her time,
The men would weep,
"So this is her when she
Gets old—impossible!" This was
Mexicali, a desert town,
Where you rode your bike,
Racing your shadow
That sometimes pulled
Ahead, other times
Fell behind. At noon,
The shadow disappeared altogether.
You smiled and asked, "Where did I go?"
You were playing
"Bicycle Thief," a boy in search
Of a job—your father's shoe store
Had failed, and myriad boxes
Of dead stock stilettos
Were stacked in your house,
Lining the hallways.
Did that many women

Dwell in the world?
And, if so, could you find them
By the scents on their throats?
By beauty marks on high cheek bones?

I think of us at the coffee shop in Fresno,
Lamenting the demise
Of the French cinema,
Both of us playing New Yorkers
In a small town. We sketched
Out our own epic features,
You the alligator tamer,
Me the linguistics professor with ink
On his hands. The special
Effects? A thumb print on the lens
And money in the bank!
But cancer knocked on your bones.
You didn't live long enough
To see Cantinflas, dead as he was,
Catch up to Woody Allen,
And those beautiful shoes
Stacked in your father's house…
Ernesto, they did find feet!
In pumps with high-heels,
Or flats with pretty little bows,
These are the women who we thought
Would curl our toes
When a director called
"Ok, boys—action!"

FROST & NERUDA

Fallen walls, barrels of apples,
Wrists caught in saws, snow, lots of snow,
And country wives stringy as chickens...
Mr. Frost, with a pipe like plumbing in his mouth,
Leads me down a leafy path.
The sage is going to tell me a story,
But first he must light a fire
For fire, he tells me, is like ice,
And ice, he says, is like fire.
Which is it? I wonder. Mr. Frost reads
My face, a rumpled sack
For last night I emptied a bag
Of cold beers into that barrel
Around my middle. "It's good
That you ask," he says, puff, puff
On his cold pipe. "But first,
Let's make a fire." A good idea,
I think. I'm wearing huaraches,
And each of my faceless toes
Could use a struck match.
But his matches are wet, all of them,
And I don't know if fire
Is ice, but I can't wait
For spring to find our bodies.

I'm in Chile, bare-chested as a pirate,
Walking with Neruda along the beach,
Picking up agates and bits of glass.
I can see a book of matches
In his shirt pocket.
He strikes one and lights
His pipe, a gift from a comrade,
No, a lover, no, a comrade lover!

I kick off my huaraches. I'm home,
I feel, salt on my eyelashes,
Salt on my lips. I ask: Master,
Why are you staring at the sea?
It must be the cosmos, or a new world order
For man and beast. He frowns at me,
Sighs, and turns when he hears a wave
Break on the beach.
Then I, minor watercolorist from
The Junior League, pull my senses together
And I see: the discarded tops
Of bikinis swaying at the edge
Of the water, little mountains
Rocking in the foam. We're quiet—
A crab with huge pinchers steps
Between us. It's early afternoon,
The wind not yet up. If we turn our backs
On the sea, we become old men
With fallen chests. If we continue staring,
We remain virile! The women
Will emerge before our eyes,
Naked and sleek as mermaids.
What is time to us?

FRIENDS

Laguna Beach, wind in the eucalyptus,
Shadows folding and unfolding in the bedroom curtains,
And I'm thinking of Ernesto in Mexico City.
What was his job? Something about oil,
Jackhammers with their shiny beaver teeth?
He wrote me a letter in longhand
And told me about his two new suits,
And the most beautiful green Peugeot.
Poor, color-blind Ernesto—really!
The car was blue.

I remember the thinness of his stationery,
Light blue as the sky,
And the airmail envelope with its rank of stripes.
Hungry for friendship, I read it four times
And then turned it the other way,
Read it through its opposite side,
And thought, I'm reading Spanish, I'm reading Esperanto,
I'm reading for clues of life in a blue—OK, green—Peugeot.
I held his letter to the light, a transparency.
A poet, he would die young,
Ink on his fingertips, ink carried over to mine.

The moon rode out on canal water,
And a tire followed. An owl swiveled its head
For one last look. I sat on the dirty bank,
Alone as ever, scared to go home—
Mother wasn't done with me. Aware
That you had to get dirty to think your life
Had meaning, I poured two scoops
Of sand on my knees. I thought: This is stupid,
And got up. The owl's eyes closed, then opened,
And I did my owl-thing, too: I closed my eyes,
And opened them to find a sofa on the canal water,
A chair, soggy books, a cookie jar, Styrofoam ice chest.
Some sneaky citizen was moving away, piece by piece,
Silently under the high white clouds—
The beginning of autumn, the valley wind snapped
Leaves on vines and the fruitless fruit trees.
One season was over, and another beginning.
This was me—age 17, done with family,
Done with the neighborhood,
With football by the glow of orange porch lights,
Though I could do with a little more of Sue,
The first girl to unpin the top button
Of her blouse for me. Where
Was she now? I bit my knuckle
And tasted its grainy salt. That's when
The red love seat came into view.
I imagined Sue with a cushion between her thighs,
And a second and third button undone,
A bra strap fallen from her shoulder.
Was I seeing right? Was she unfurling her finger
And beckoning me to come along? Like the owl,
I blinked and said: "Who? Who?"
It couldn't possibly be me
Who looked headed nowhere fast?

SOAP OPERA

If she had looked in my pocket,
Mom would have found nine marbles
And a drain plug attached to a chain,
Maybe a sunflower seed,
Certainly the tongue depressors I found behind the pharmacy.
No, Mom was watching *As the World Turns*,
And waiting for the commercial
Before she would get the belt to make me dance
The dance of the disobedient child.

I was late for lunch.
Poor me, I hadn't looked up from playing
To know that it was twelve-thirty, that my family
Of starved gladiators was tearing flesh from last night's chicken.
I entered the house and hurried to my bedroom,
My three brothers clearing out
When they heard the commercial start.
I put on my long pants to lessen the pain,
And danced when the belt began
To sing at my knees. Then it stopped,
And Mom said, *Estupido*, I'm missing my show!

I wiped away tears,
Dabbed spit where the belt got through.
I shuddered and lifted my head.
In the living room, another commercial started—
Sixty seconds for another ditty from the belt?

On the floor I brought out my loot for the day,
The tongue depressors and marbles with their hypnotic stares.
A tear fell on my wrist. How I wished the house
Would fill with them.

It would take ten years before
I could pull the chain
And watch them all go down.

HANDS

In a scary movie,
A severed hand crept a few inches,
Stopped, index finger in air,
And turned crab-like toward the audience.
That's when I got up from my velvety chair
In the matinee and moved two rows
Back, then three more when I peeked
Between my fingers and saw a hand
Moving toward us kids. I closed my eyes
When a girl—no, me!—screamed
As the organ moaned, a prelude
To the appearance of more severed parts?
I said nothing when I opened my eyes
And saw the hand on my knee.
I blinked. How did it crawl
From the screen and settle with a pinch
On my jeans? I looked up—a bald usher
Next to me, a finger in his mouth.
I jumped from that chair and hurried,
Shirttail out, for the lobby door.

Saturday, sometime in the early sixties,
Fear only cost a grubby dime.

A SIMPLE PLAN

for V.M.

To get rid of
A dog, you put on
Your brother's shoes,
Slip into a shirt
Hanging on a nail
In the garage,
Smack Dad's hair oil
Into your dirty locks,
The scent of confusion.
You call, Let's go, boy,
And with the
Dog's neck in
A clothesline noose,
You follow your skinny shadow
Down the street
And cut through
A vacant lot,
Same place
Where you stepped
On a board with a nail
And whimpered home,
The board stuck
Like a ski to your shoe.
You walk past
The onion field,
Little shrunken heads
Hiding hot, unshed tears,
And stop at the canal.
The dog laps water,
Nibbles a thorn from his paw,
And barks at a toad
In the oiled weeds.

The sun's razor
Is shining at your throat,
And wind ruffles
Your splayed hair,
Where a hatchet
Would fit nicely—
You feel the sharpened
Edge of guilt.
Come on, boy
You say, and leap
On slippery rocks
Set in the canal.
You stop to
Look inside an abandoned
Car with a pleated grill—
Three bullet holes in the door
On the driver's side.
You think, Someone
Drove this car
Here and killed it.

You brave another mile.
When you arrive,
The dog prances with
Joy. What is it?
A jackrabbit in
The brush? Feral cat
Or stink birds? You pick up
A board, one just a little
Smarter than the one
That nailed you with pain.
With all your strength,
You hurl it end over
End. The dog knows
What to do. He runs
After it. Time for you to spin

On your heels and, arms
Kicked up at your side,
Lungs two bushes
Of burning fire,
Get back home.
That night it's steaks
On a grill, a celebration
Because someone
In the family won
A two-hundred-dollar lottery.
You eat to the bone
And then nearly
Choke on the gristle.
You drag your full
Belly to the front
Yard, and stake
Yourself on the lawn.
The neighbor's porch light
Bursts on, and a shooting
Star cuts across the sky—
You touch your throat
And think, Something just died.
You lay with hands
Laced behind your head.
Somewhere up
The block a dog barks.
My dog is out there,
You think, and behind
Your closed eyes
You see him, a nail
In his bloody paw,
A board in his mouth,
And shooting stars
Passing over the curves
Of his wet pupils.
If you were a better person,

You would stab
Your own foot
And let him pick up a scent
Back home.

The science teacher with dyed hair was set for a doctor's exam at four. He asked, "Do you know what a polyp is?" I shrugged my shoulders. He placed his ancient hand on his stomach and lowered it to his intestines where, in my appraisal of body functions, I thought shit begins. I left his office, promising to look up polyp and learn most of the periodic table by Friday. Under a tree on campus, I pulled an apple from my backpack—solid roughage, a good intestinal scrubber. I was fourteen, in summer school because I smacked Larry Austin with a catcher's mitt, his tiny head fitting so nicely in the sweet spot. I thought that by the end of the day I would be wiser by one word—*polyp*. My science teacher, I now see, was in his early forties, a good man. I wish I could have learned the periodic table—one more failed promise. The last time I saw my teacher he was getting into his car. His head was down, his white roots showing. I could tell he was trying to survive—he had two hours before his exam and he was eating an apple right down to its bitter core.

EARNED & UNEARNED PENNIES

When Uncle Joe woke on the couch
The spark of pain in his back was gone.
So was some of his hair but he didn't mind.
He massaged the Mt. Rushmore of his knuckles—
No pain there. Full of happiness,
He swallowed three prunes like goldfish.

I visited old Uncle Joe after a mighty wind
Rocked leaves from his fruit trees.
Down the porch and farting
Every third step, he said,
"By thirty, I lost most of my hair,
Plus my hearing. The teeth might have gone
Too, if I hadn't learned to shut up." He
Pressed three pennies into my palm,
And said, "This is what I earned
When I first poked a broom into a doorway."
The wide part of the bamboo rake
Hid my yawn—immigrant story, one from 1916,
Which for me, a boy of nine,
Was just before the dinosaurs kicked off
And blended into dark, sludgy oil.
He asked, "Did I ever tell you about the tank
That ran over the tip of my left boot?"
In WWII he went in a private
And came out a private. I said
Behind my rake, "Yeah, Uncle, lot of times."
With that, he pried open my palm
And snatched back the pennies.

I raked leaves and broke open an orange.
I was on my last slice when
Uncle returned with the coins.

He said I needed a good start in life
And asked how far I would go
With all the money he pressed on me.
Smart-aleck me, I pointed with
The rake and said, "'bout the edge
Of the lawn, maybe the orange tree."
He fumed and worked his dentures
Upside down, like fangs.
I said, "Ah, Uncle, just kidding!"
When he approached, claws out.
He caught my wrist, yanked,
And yelled in Spanish, then Portuguese,
"You wait! You're not going to keep
Your teeth! Or these!" He opened my palm,
And, for a second time, the pennies
Rolled back into the leathery pouch
Of his tightfisted hand.

ORPHANS

First Mother moved away,
Driving off in an old VW,
Smoke like little fists when she popped the clutch.

Joey ate his mush, he dressed himself,
One sock blue, the other black—
That was close enough.

Then Father, done with a game of solitaire,
Scooted his chair from the kitchen table.
"I got to get some air," he announced.
He watered the rose bush in the yard
And then drove away, his face
A small walnut in the rearview mirror.

Joey turned over his father's deck—
A black ace, a red jack of diamonds, a deuce of clubs,
Nothing really. "Why," he asked,
"Why did they leave me?"

He walked himself to school
And returned home with grass in his hair.
Joey, the orphan, refilled his bowl with mush.
Twilight entered the house.
The cat left by the back door, his slugged profile on the fence.

It was all planned, Joey thought in bed.
First mother would leave, then father.
In sleep, they returned to him—
They were at the beach, Father with a seashell to his ear,
Mother waving at a boat hoisting sail.

Family does that.
They go away, then blame you for not visiting,
Then fault you when you do.
They wash ashore in terrible dreams.

RUSSIAN PORK, 1962

The Russians sent up sputnik,
Then sent over a team to film a family in the Fresno projects,
The Morenos, all tidy and sitting down
To a typical dinner—macaroni with weenies,
Tumblers of Kool-Aid, a salad that resembled
The grass plucked from our hair at day's end.
Loud as pirates, they ate as if with hammer and sickle
From mismatched bowls close to their faces. Mr. Moreno,
Bald as Comrade Khrushchev, turned an eye to the camera.
He hammered his fist on the table, "We don't go to church
But when we do, we're Catholic!" The family all pounded
With their hammers and sickles, and whooped.
Bobby chewed open-mouthed
For the camera, and asked for seconds, then thirds,
More Kool-Aid. Then he had to be hung upside down
By his dad—Bobby had been chewing gum
With his macaroni-and-cheese.

I swear this is true, a sputnik did go up
And the Russians arrived in large black cars.
These men in dark suits opened and closed
Every door in the house, as if spying
On a low-class American family. What were
These Russians trying to learn from the Morenos?
The secret of survival in the atomic age?
After all, a father couldn't always be there
To pound gum and macaroni-and-cheese from a child's throat.

I swear the cameras rolled, the men wore black.
We kids, pigeon-chested and bare footed,
Stood at the front window, breathing on the glass,
Fogging up the family's revelry in dessert.
We waited for them to crush those sputnik jawbreakers,

The candy of our time, and for the family of nine
To come out. We wanted their autographs,
These movie stars, these unkillable, project kids.

TEETH MARKS

I didn't like my chances for success.
Stepfather was in the living room,
A shot glass on the TV tray of dead
And live presidents, a shot glass positioned
On the face of Herbert Hoover. I asked
My hands, "Why this family?"
The girl I liked a lot had moved away,
Taking with her the pencil I lent her for our history final.
The pencil, I remember, was gnawed by my teeth,
And the eraser was mostly gone. God, how I was forced
To correct my mistakes—Spanish
Subjunctives, the English ones—
And how pitifully I rendered one-cell organisms
On a piece of unlined paper. I knew then—the moon
Had shrugged itself from the branches—my sadness involved
This girl. Where was she? Where was my pencil?
Clacking between her top and bottom front teeth?
Or maybe she was making loopy script
In her diary and writing—my heart thumped—about me!

In my bedroom, I turned our glow-in-the-dark Christ
Toward the wall, unbuckled my belt,
And did what sixteen-year-olds do in thirty-three seconds.
In ecstasy I pictured that girl with the pencil in her mouth,
Gnawing away, adding her own teeth marks.
She licked that lead point, came up now
To say it wasn't so bad, an embarrassing dribble
On her chin dark as first-time sin.

The teacher—his tie the color of a yellow tooth,
His pace the pace of a Daddy-Longlegs spider—
Was drilling for what could be oil reserves in our thick heads.

I grew thirsty learning that in 1920 our valley lake
Was drained for more farm land—
Mr. Worthy pulled the plug on the Tulare.
What were we going to drink now?

He was teaching us California geography,
Why, I didn't know. The class was biology,
Where even the squeamish opened frogs
Like coin purses.

The teacher smiled,
His teeth matching his tie.
His spidery hands came together in a chapel.
"Now, class," he asked, "What is the capital of California?"

I was thinking of frogs heaped in cold storage
When Steve raised his hand,
His wrist inked with answers for an English test next period.
"Los Angeles," he said, then shifted his eyes
When he saw the yellow smile disappear.
"No, no, I mean San Francisco—that's it!"

I knew the capital was Sacramento—
Stepfather had gotten a flat there on a country road,
And we spent three hours watching the geese winging south,
Their eyes narrowed for the glint of water.

Did the geese grow thirsty?
Maybe the geese had to circle until they dropped.

They were cheated out of a lake, but we ignorant
Cheats—Steve with answers dripping
On his sweaty wrists—got to sit in chairs.

I thought, then, of the rubbery frog,
How when I finally took a knife to its belly,
One of its tiny stiff arms pointed at me.

NELSON, MY DOG

Like the cat he scratches the flea camping in fur.
Unlike the cat he delights in water up to his ears.
He frolics. He catches a crooked stick—
On his back he naps with legs straight up in the air.
Nelson shudders awake. He responds to love
From head to tail. In happiness
His front legs march in place
And his back legs spark when they push off.
On a leash he knows his geography.
For your sake he looks both ways before crossing,
He sniffs at the sight of a poodle trimmed like a hedge,
And he trots the street with you second in command.
In the park, he ponders a squirrel attached to a tree
And he shovels a paper cup on his nose.
He sweeps after himself with his tail,
And there is no hand that doesn't deserve a lick.
Note this now, my friends:
Nelson can account the heritage of heroic dogs:
One, canines lead the blind,
Two, they enter fire to rescue the child and the child's toy,
Three, they swim for the drowning,
Four, they spring at the thief,
Five, they paddle ponds for the ball that got away,
Six, for the elderly they walk side by side to the very end,
Seven, they search for bones but stop when called,
Eight, they bring mud to all parties,
Nine, they poke among the ruins of a burnt house,
Ten, they forgive what you dish out on a plate.

Nelson is a companion, this much we know,
And if he were a movie star, he would do his own stunts—
O, how he would fly, climb the pant legs of a scoundrel
And stand tall rafting on white-water rivers!

He has befriended the kingdom of animals:
He once ran with wolves but admittedly not very far,
He stepped two paces into a cave and peeked at the bear,
He sheltered a kitten,
He righted the turtle pedaling its stumps on its back,
Under the wheeling stars he caravanned with the mule,
He steered sheep over a hill,
He wisely let the skunk pass,
He growled at the long-bearded miser,
He joined ducks quacking with laughter,
Once he leaped at a pheasant but later whined from guilt.

Nelson's black nose is a compass in the wilds.
He knows nature. He has spied spires of summer smoke,
He circled cold campfires,
He howled at a gopher and scratched at the moon,
He doctored his wounds with his tongue,
He has pawed a star of blood left in snow.
He regards the fireplace, the embers like blinking cats,
This too we know about Nelson.
True, he is sometimes tied to parking meters
And sometimes wears the cone of shame from the vet's office.
But again, he is happiness.
He presents his belly for a friendly scratch.
If you call him, he will drop his tennis ball,
Look up, and come running,
This muddy friend for life. When you bring your nose
To his nose for something like a kiss,
You can find yourself in his eyes.

PART TWO

BEAN PLANTS

You say you were four and suffering insomnia,
That you lay in bed and sometimes crept
To look at your brother, then returned
To struggle with the sheets, thumb in your mouth
For the taste of something solid. You say it was summer,
That you could smell the iron-scent
Ruins of the junkyard next to the house,
And then pick up the scent of wet straw—
Down the alley, a factory was making brooms.
You were four, and already thinking about the past.
It was you, wasn't it, who planted beans
Into the yard and jumped up and down
When the plants unraveled from their crumbs of earth?
And it was you who created the waterworks for their survival,
For the survival of ants, too, because didn't they require
The smallest bead of moisture?
You watched that little patch of beans,
And every other day watched your neighbor hang laundry,
A clothespin in her mouth. You spied her from your
Back porch, scared and certain that the clothespin
Would pinch her tongue. You pinched your own
Pink nub, jumped off the porch,
And started off to Charlie's Market—
Bright you, you suddenly remembered the nickel in your pocket.
Before you crossed Van Ness Avenue
You stopped to pull up a snapdragon at the edge
Of your yard and thought, It's kind of like a clothespin.
You worked its mouth open and closed. All the while
You were thinking of the past, the week before,
When you pulled up another flower that bled white—
Your brother, the cruel one, said that was
Where cows got their milk. It was OK,
He said, to drink that kind of flowery milk.

When you licked the milky stem, he jumped up and down
And shouted that you were a stupid cow, then
Changed his mind to say that at least cows
Ate grass, but stupid you, you liked to eat dirt.
You soured your face as you spit and spit
And, as you remember, went home to get
A whipping for something you couldn't remember.
But that was in the past, the week before, and now
You were standing on the corner of your yard,
The snapdragon in your fingers. You dropped the flower
And crossed the street to the store,
Where Charlie was reading a newspaper—a monkey
Had gone to space, he told you from behind
A wreath of cigarette smoke. How come the monkey
Is there? *There* was front page news.
The old Armenian shook his head, took your nickel
And you left with a bag of M&Ms.
You crossed the street and sat behind a stack of boards,
Out of sight of your brother. You ate your favorite red ones,
Then the green ones, and saved the rest.
Back home you got another whipping
For a bathtub ring and then took your shuddering body
To the yard where the bean plants stood in the dirt.
You watered them, beads of moisture clinging to their leaves,
And then said, Leave me alone,
When Donald, a boy up the alley, climbed onto the fence
And said he had something to show you.
He unraveled his fist: it was an army man with his head gone.
Donald said that he had melted it by holding it over the stove,
And then you remembered why you had gotten
Your whipping the week before—
The burnt heads of matches in your pocket!
Donald said that his father had killed two chickens,
And if you wanted to look at their heads
And feet you had better hurry. By then
You were no longer crying. Your face

Was dirty, the rivers of grime on your palms dark.
You don't remember Donald leaving,
Or dinner, or the junkman locking in his yard.
But you remember your mother applying lipstick
To see a neighbor, and your brother jumping on the couch
And screaming, I'm going into space!
That's when you stopped coloring fire on a piece of paper,
All the blood you had ever seen packed tightly
In that crayon in your fist. You asked, What's it mean—space?
He asked, What do you mean, Stupid,
It's up in the sky! Don't you know?
You looked up and made your eyes really big
As if their enormity could give
You the power to see beyond the ceiling.

Then night came, bed with its strangled sheets, and insomnia.
You fit a thumb into your mouth.
You wondered if the monkey was ever coming down
From space. You stood at the window
With your M&Ms. The junkyard was quiet,
But beyond it you could hear the roar of the freeway.
You were the four-year-old who when he
Couldn't sleep would think of the past.
This much you knew,
Plus that space was above your head
And was what Mom called heaven.
You had to be good if you wanted to reach it,
You remember her saying.
You put a brown M&M into your mouth, let it melt,
And scooted its sweetness over your molars.
You made out in the yard the arms of your bean plants
Throwing themselves up to get more light,
Even if the light was from the porch. You went back
To bed and placed your hands over your head:
How sorry you were for the bean plants eating dirt,
With their skinny arms always raised and so tired.

PASTORAL

The tumbleweed gathers up rumors
And rolls out of town. Yanked-up roots are piled beyond the barn,
And even now a fly with octagonal eyes
Is sipping coolant pooled under the tractor.

"Mr. Goto," my father-in-law tells me in the yard,
"The doctor said he needed more exercise.
He got a bike."

Stars squeeze their icy light,
A June bug hisses on the screen door,
And a family of possums wades in the cistern.
Far east, clouds are throwing lightning on some poor devil.

"Yeah, Mr. Goto, had 40 acres of walnuts,"
My father-in-law says. Red coal of his cigarette
In the dark, a pause for the chickens to stop their mad fluttering.
"He got run over last week. I don't know about his bike."

Mid-May. The irrigated cotton rows lit with moonlight.
Three months, and the heat will bring us inside.
For now, we take to the road on bikes,
The Buddhist wheels spinning front and back.

It's Sunday morning.
The last white man turns black at the alley's end.
If he marched with his arms swinging,
The right sleeve of his jacket would fall off.
He's that poor.

Michael, the security, blinks his flashlight against his palm—
It's something to do. Business has taken a day off.
The bananas fall out of their skins.
Apples soften. In the closed meat shop
The tinker-toy snout of a pig drools,
And the ropes of chorizo are big enough to skip through.
Mexican music makes you want you rub your eyes
For a good cry.

You can walk on glass, suffer,
And hear, "*Oye, carnal*, got soda money for me?"
The *vato* is sitting on a stripped bike, going nowhere.

But there's the tinkle of a bell on a store door.
There's laughter coming from Suki's Nails and Feet.
And look at Javier, with glue and paper,
Making *piñatas* behind a chain-link fence—
The beer-bellied Spider-Man will take a birthday beating.

A breeze twists through the trees,
One jammed meter throws up its expired red flag.
When the bell at the Mexican Baptist Church sounds,
Huge black birds fed on dropped burgers honk from wires.
They bow their heads and cast shadows over feral cats.

What is meant by escape?
You could be any dog hugging an ancient building for shade.
When you turn the corner, the knife-bright sun cuts ruthlessly
The shadow from your already mangy body.

On top of an overturned tub, the back of a wagon,
On shoulders even, Lizarras and Yamaguchi of JMLA[1],

Yelled in Spanish and Japanese,
Go barefoot before you buy from the company store.

Maybe the flat palms of clouds went east
On the power of lightning and the thunder of strikers,

Maybe Mr. Oxnard with his big sugar acreage,
With his factory, helped himself to another sausage.

The *Oxnard Courier* called the union: "grim band
Of fellows, lower class of Japanese and Mexicans."

But working beets was grim,
All right pay at daybreak and down to grimy coins at dusk.

You had to be more than low class to salt your rice
Or tortilla with a rich man's dirt. And so what

If newspapers wrote: "Mexicans with knives..."
You would think every Juan or Ramon staggered

With thirteen blades sticking from his body,
Any one of them good enough to whittle

Mr. Oxnard's earth from under fingernails.
But guns, not knives, were used,

A shotgun with its double promise of a quick heaven,
On the morning of March 23. Sixteen men

Hurt, mule and horse, one child
With the stigmata in the left palm—poorly aimed pistol

Shots from a buckaroo deputy. All the while,
Mrs. Oxnard was coming down the steps

Of one grand staircase, her skirts swishing,
Her pretty little mouth greeting, "Good morning,

Good morning." Flowers were on the table.
A cube of sugar from her sugar daddy

Sank like a rock into her morning tea.

---

1 JMLA, Japanese-Mexican Labor Association

Arturo stomps the heel of his boot and tells me:
Every *pinche* minute I mess up a red ant. That's no good,

I say to the young man in the next row,
The shadow of my hoe cutting weeds in Boswell's beet field.

Arturo says: every super *pinche* half-hour I see this squirrel spin
And drop—you know, the chemicals you and me are breathing.

That's not nice, I tell him and hold my breath for a long second.
I then feel something on my sleeve—

Sunlight where there was dark and the icy thread of stars.
We started before dawn, as the tainted valley wind nudged us along

And I had no thoughts other than counting my steps.
Now morning has peeled its eye open. Black birds follow

Our shoeprints, scolding us with hard, clapper-like tongues.
My anger is fired up by weeds and black birds in their judges' robes,

And the shouting at my house
Where we five kids grow like weeds ourselves,

Cut down by the anger of mother's hot iron,
A stepfather's glare through a shot glass licked of bourbon.

I think of home, far to the east
And remember the sea that I once heard when I put a can to my ear

And heard a storm I liked. Then a black bird shouts
And Arturo, steps ahead, says: every morning I say my *pinche* prayers

And I'm still in hell. He spits words I can't make out, or care about.
I stop when the long tooth of my hoe divides

One of those thin-waisted red ants. I stop, hunch down,
And study its jaws still gripping its load.

Poor guy, I think. This halved red ant is still kicking.
Righted, his legs circle the whorls of my fingerprints.

I raise his back legs onto my knuckle
And notice even in death you keep going.

I painted a wall of a farm house
And then watched a shadow crawl up the wall,
Dirtying my work. Who would hire me?
I told myself and sat on the porch
To eat a sandwich and free grapes
From the vine. It was 103,
The sun knife-bright. I felt a necklace
Of sweat break pearl by pearl from
Under my chin. I ate, drank water,
And then gazed at a *campesino* stumbling
From the vines, a grape pan in his hand.
It was high noon on that eighty-acre vineyard,
And somewhere a dog was barking.
I got up, the latches of my own knees hurting.
I called, *Oye, señor!* His shirttail
Was out, a flag of defeat, and his knees
Were muddy from cutting grapes.
I approached him. I said in Spanish,
My mother-in-law made this sandwich.
The bottled water didn't need to be explained.
He took both, releasing a black smile.
His front teeth were gone, his dreamy hope
For clean work absolutely gone.
I then shivered in that sun: he was my age,
Early fifties, and who was I facing
But my immigrant self. He turned
And started toward the closest row.
I moved beneath the shadows of a pine tree,
Hands on hips, thinking, He's me,
He's not me. The grape fields
Fluttered their leaves. Nothing cooled.
By the time I picked up my paintbrush
And climbed the gallows of tottering ladder.

We each had our job, mine two feet higher,
And he, this *campesino*, was bowing
Under a vine, his knees hitting the sandy
Ground, genuflecting to the powers
Of a hot summer sun.

I was made of flesh, not fur
Or tail, not paws thick as leather.
I bent down, patted his coat,
And I asked, "Is it time now?"
The old stray was reddish brown,
His breathing shallow,
And his tail a short whip against my leg.
"Is it time now?" I repeated,
Thinking of that journey
Down the tractor path,
He keeping pace to the left of me.
But first, he licked the drops
From a leaky faucet,
And I tied my shoes,
These twin boats scuffed
From my anger kicking the world.
When I called him, he followed me
To the end of the vineyard,
The grapes puny on the vines.
If I stuck my hand
In among the sulfured leaves,
Spiders would pull in their legs
And rabbits leap away.
I tossed a clod among the vines
And watched the lift of a blackbird,
The undertaker's favorite.
I walked to the end of the first row
And the dog, my future, followed
With his tags clinking.
It was sunset, or nearly sunset.
My shirt ruffled in the valley wind
That shuffles our shoeprints—
Every day we stamped our place

In this sandy soil,
And the wind wiped our tracks clean.
I looked back. I saw a house
Among vineyards, my wife pinning wash.
I had done much, done little,
And my shirts on the line
Had more wind in them than I did.
I crumbled a clod. I sniffed the air,
And the dog sniffed,
Nose pointed skyward.
What were we smelling on a fall day
But our years dying on the mortgaged vines?

THE MIXTECA'S HONORED GUEST

para José Padilla

Throw open the window,
Whip a rug and let the knuckles of boiling water
Become tea.

Hang the killed pig from a tree,
Permit the frijoles to troop into a pot
And stand aside when the rooster screams
At my hatchet-faced woman.

Jose viene hoy!

Pile ice in a tub, bottled beer like yellowish glow of lanterns,
And that oil stain on the back patio, scrub it!
If the dog comes, chain him.
If the neighbor looks over the fence,
Inquire about tomatoes.

Jose viene hoy!

Pray that the sky clears,
The embers of a blinking cat warm our feet—
It's March and the sky will burn a star for us, a good sign.

Honored guest, *licenciado*,
We'll set the pig's snout and tail on a plate—
The front will know the back for the first time.

Jose viene hoy!

In a field, my boy trapped *chapulines*, grasshoppers,
Which I'll stir in oil—radio on the sill
Is crying a ranchera one last time!

We'll set these armored insects, wing-to-wing,
Before him. What use is a fork, a tortilla?
He has only to part his lips,
And these treats will fly into his mouth.

Thirty years ago
The Irish and Italians
Were up on scaffolds
With trowels slinging
Mud at walls.
They shot staples
Into two-by-fours,
Sometimes into
Their ring fingers,
A marriage
To a job
That would bring them
To their knees?

Now it's Mexicanos,
The sing-song Spanish
Of Morelia.
The scaffolds tremble
Under their boots—
A Javier or an Ernesto,
A cousin of a cousin,
Got them these jobs.
Lonche, the *jefe* calls.
They eat sandwiches,
Legs dangling
Over the sides.

It was a hard
Climb over
A border fence
Then, whistling,
Up thirteen floors.
Pigeon-toed

They hold on,
The wind pushing
Front and back—
Politicians, too...

Once upon a time there were five brothers.
One handled a leaf blower,
The second pumped his hands in dishwater,
The third hoed cotton,
The fourth raised roofs for a man named Levi,

And the fifth, the youngest,
Rounded up chickens in the State of Zacatecas.

The oldest brother sent letters,
And within them
Photos of their cars, all used—
A Toyota Tacoma for the first,
An Altima for the second,
For the third and fourth,
Born eight months apart, Ford Tempos,
Four-bangers that dropped parts.

The fifth brother was jealous.
Left behind to work the farm,
His ride was a bicycle and sometimes a jalopy truck.

Then their letters from the states arrived asking for money—
Their cars were stolen, impounded for unpaid tickets,
Dented in parking lots, insured but for what,
And, *hijole*, the gas!

By lamplight the fifth brother assessed his good fortune—
The soles of his huaraches were his tires,
His heart his engine, the blood in his veins his transmission line,
His eyes headlights, his gold teeth his grill,

And his stops at the post office
A conversation, maybe more, with the flowery women,
Idling.

"I could take a cup of lard from your cheeks,
And cook with it," the wife said to
Her shirtless husband. They were eating
Watermelon in the side yard,
Away from the sun that staggered everyone
From six until six when it went
Down like a plane behind the trees.
The flies packed it in,
But the mosquitoes, those druggies
In search of a vein, hovered near the garden hose.
The husband laughed. He bit into his melon
And chewed. She said, "I could take
A pail to your belly and feed all the county."
The old man laughed. He said,
"Dorothy, I still love your feet." At that,
She wiggled her toes, and said,
"I'm gonna get me a toe ring like the young girls.
Gonna dye my hair, do my eyes blue,
And pull on a miniskirt." Even after
Thirty years, after this business
Of her taking cups and pails to his flesh,
He handed her a second slice
Of icy melon. He said, "Honey,
You got a mosquito on your neck."
She slapped that whiny creature,
And then slapped her knee
For him to come and sit.
This he did, but not his full weight.
That would be later when
The moon, big ole' Peeping Tom,
Stared through the bedroom window.
He would undress, splash himself
With something nice from the shelf,
And expend a teaspoon of lard for their pleasure.

I had been waiting all my life
To be fed and cooled by air conditioning,
And to climb into bed where a woman slept,
Her breathing so natural I had no heart to wake her
And ask, "Do we have bread?" I had in mind
A large sandwich piled with meats and cheese,
A tomato bursting from its seams. So I took
Off my shirt, the hairs on my chest like antennas.
So I lay next to her, a sheet over us, the room morgue-cold.
To warm myself up I started to whistle
"The Bridge on the River Kwai." She woke,
Touched me down below, and said, "Big sausage boy."
I was chewing on a carrot, having already devoured
A chilly slice of melon. I cleared my throat
And joked, "You're always thinking about food."
When she turned away, I thought,
Oh, idiot boy, you said the wrong thing.
I envisioned the air conditioner sighing to a stop,
The lunch meat curling up like the tips of shoes,
And me out on the street again,
My breeze the revolving blades of a push mower—
A summer job that would go on forever.
Then she purred and arched her bottom,
A lovely globe against my flesh. Then I learned:
Not always, just sometimes, when a woman
Turns away in bed, it's for you to put down
Your carrot, use both hands, and take
Hold from a different angle.

THIS TIME

I see us at the river bend
At Piedra, a blanket on the rocky shore,
And a hawk—or what I believe was a hawk—
Circling. A cool autumn, drifts of leaves,
And on the surface of the river driftwood set free.

We watched the driftwood slowly pass,
Kissed because it was something to do,
And in the sand in front of our blanket I drew the house
Where we would live. No artist, it was a little crooked,
And over this house a hawk, rough dots that I said were stars,
And an antenna on the roof—
Wind came up and softened the edges.

We were young, the morning sun shining on a willow.
How I wish the driftwood would pass again,
This time even more slowly.

A WALK IN A COUNTY PARK

The walk in the park proved beautiful
As you discovered ducks waddling in a line,
Following an orderly instinct
While everyone around you—friends, family,
Your mates in their cubicles at work—knew
Nothing of order. This was the first week in fall,
Three days before your boss with fossilized veins
From head to toe had called you
In and crunched a breath mint
To make the news sweeter—
You were out of a job, you the sentry
At the supply cabinet
And main man at the paper shredder.
Now this Saturday walk. You touched your heart
And proclaimed, "I love nature!"
As you groaned up a path and through
The swinging doors of ferns closed behind you.
The trees cast cold shadows. "The ducks!"
You cried, "I get to see my little friends!"
Your heart sped up. But you absently stopped
To praise the clouds—little did you know
That boiling thunder would discharge
Lightning onto good and bad children.
Then you remembered order,
Remembered the ducks on the other side
Of the river, all in a line. You got going.
You stepped into that cold, ancient current
Determined to follow the ducks.
You were a sudden naturalist with burrs
And seedy fibers sticking to the cuffs
Of your pants. Then you stopped
And saw: the ducks were not ducks
But white plastic bags of sand set against

The muddy bank. It was all gone,
The beautiful fall day. You had to have
Something. You waited for your heart to slow
Before you petted the top of a sand bag.
If it had been one of the ducks,
That's where its head would have been,
Its beak clacking at your loving hand.

GLOBAL WARMING

After the late news,
I walked along

A river, the good air
In my nostrils

Replaced with
Something dead,

A raccoon or possum?
The sky was

Filled with stars
But what of them,

Or what of Boy Scouts
Planting trees?

What of the maestro
In tails

Or the witticism
The greatest

Thing in America
Is Europe?

Suddenly my heart leapt.
On the river

I spotted a polar bear,
White and huge.

Had the glaciers
Melted? Would the

Penguins soon show
Up for the last

Cocktail hour?
I slid down

The river bank and saw
On a closer look

I was wrong—the river's
Current was pushing

A white refrigerator,
Fallen from a pickup

In broad daylight?
That used monster

Of an appliance
Floated past, ice cube

Trays kicking inside.
Late news over,

The morning paper
Hours away. I walked

Back to the house,
The smelly air

Of the future
Coming from us.

POLICE STATE

I had faith in dogs
Until a husky pointed and said,

"That's him." I was carrying a translation
Of a revolutionary poet

In my heart. I touched
My heart and asked, "You mean me?"

The husky pointed again
And the cops frisked me,

Patting twice around my heart,
Suspicious because

My heartbeats were hot and loud,
Evidence that I had gotten the translation right?

"Where do you live?" a cop asked.
I could have told this badge

The clouds, in my frothy dreams,
In a townhouse at the edge

Of the Gaza strip.
I could have told him

A pile of wood shavings,
Under a tree, or

Possibly in the vapors
Of a heaven

That lets everyone in.
No, smart me, answered, "I live

In a house, sir"—a mistake.
For the first time

In my life I climbed
In the back of a cop car.

We drove noiselessly
Until the radio squawked—

The small tragedy of a boy
With his head

Caught between the slats
Of a picket fence.

We drove over
And they pulled him out,

Then let me free—
The sole of my left shoe

Was flapping
And I would cost the county

Money if they brought me in.
But the dog,

That traitor, caught up
And unleashed a couple of fleas

That had me scratching,
Punishment for

Hoarding poetry in my heart?
I was making my getaway

When I stopped to rip
The bothersome sole from my shoe.

A parrot, the neighborhood watch
Perched in the window,

Ordered, "Keep moving, buddy,
Keep moving."

OLD GENT AT HYDE PARK

Here comes the flat foot in search of its match,
Here comes a wart, the sagging chin,
Here comes breath retreating from a lung.

(Playing an old man on a bench,
you bring a slice of toast for the birds—
damn picky brood wing over to the woman with a French roll.)

Here comes the hearing aid full of gossip,
Here comes the dog, the three-pronged cane,
Here comes a white hair for the nose that fell over.

(Eyeing the woman with the French roll
you think, She sees me as a tree. You would smile
but you left your teeth in a turkey drumstick three years before.)

Here comes Nothing, here comes Half-Past Four,
Here comes the fart as you rise from the bench,
And the children, little fucks, crying, Mister, do that again!

(Shaking your cane at them, you oblige.)

THE SALT OF TWO OLD FRIENDS, NOW DEAD

Everyone I knew turned
And collapsed into piles of salt,
The stuff of hypertension and thirst.
The phone is dead, the wife gone,
The calico cat in the tree. I pick up
The phone, put it back down.
It's this activity, pick up
And put back, that leads finally
To my lunch of a dry sandwich,
A pickle that I view strangely
As an olive branch. What kind
Of peace am I looking for?
I eat lunch, pace the living room
And tap the window—
My cat in the tree dissolves into salt.
No, he's just leaped from
The branch. I stare at the phone
And know there's a prophet in there
Preaching a clearance on headstones.
When it finally rings,
I pick up and lick the point of my pencil,
Ready to take notes, and answer,
"Hello, hello, is it one of you?"
The sound of an oven door opening,
A footstep, hands scrubbed under a faucet...
I pound the phone against my palm
And the salt of their dead lives
Pours from the little holes.

The wheelbarrow is dark at morning,
And dime-bright at noon.
A hawk hovers, wind stirs leaves
And dog prints. The rafters
Of the barn bang. I drink
Iced tea on the porch,
And think of the bushels
Of air in my lungs, of the blood
Draining from my heart,
Of the rusty pulleys
Inside my legs. I thumb
A gnat from my tea,
And I recognize its face,
Little whiner that was
A student years ago.
I rub it on my jeans.
I look down at an ant
With big cargo in its mouth,
Something like a piano
If it was my mouth.
I don't crush him like the gnat.
Instead, when I get up
With the help of those pulleys,
Blood, air, I'm careful.
Off the porch and in the tractor path,
My feet, I see, are splayed,
Not unlike my choice of
Where I should live—
City or country?
When I walk, it's the erratic
Trail of a hurt ant,
A great thumb pressing down
From the clear sky.

FORTUNE

Da Vinci, I think, said, When Fortune comes,
Hang on to her locks, for I tell you
She's bald in the back. And as for me,
I'm bald front and back.
My toupee would float off like an island
If I jumped into the hotel pool.
I keep dry. I'm on the road,
Doing Mark Twain just before he died.
And I almost died in Omaha
While I watched a rerun of 1990 Miss America
And Miss Nebraska's tiny majorette skirt rode up.
She smoothed it down, cut a sharp glance
At America and, with those shampooed locks bouncing,
Returned to twirling her fiery batons.
I swallowed my drink. My bushy eyebrows
Crawled up like centipedes. The next day
In Fargo, a small lake rippled lines
Better than the ones I delivered on stage.

Bankers and CEOs may want more—
Rat-like, they'll claw at Fortune's hair to see
If the babe's really bald. What then?
And what of me, now that I'm back on tour.
I have lost confidence. My voice is the squeak
Of an actor speaking through a toilet roll.
My eyebrows descended, even bushier,
And the saggy skin on my throat could go
To a burn victim. On Groundhog Day
My shadow will make its escape. For now,
It's December in Kearney, Nebraska,
Another icy lake, this one not delivering rippled lines
But a frozen gaze. When I peer down,

The ice throws back the reflection
Of a man with a hangover,
And frost in his beard that won't melt in spring.

L.A. SCENE AT A RESTAURANT CALLED "ONE"

"I'm a conceptual artist," he says,
And shows me, a violinist, the fingernails of his left hand—
Brittle scenes of the Seine River in its four seasons.

I'm drinking a California champagne,
Little bubbles applauding at the lip of the glass,
Not unlike the clamor of my last Beethoven Sonata #4—
To hide the hundred no-shows,
Ten friends in the audience forced up a thousand faces.

"They look real," I say, and, sipping, destroy the applause,
My Happy Hour pleasure at $8.75 a glass.

"You should grow your nails longer," I suggest.
"Do scenes of Twain's Mississippi, the Grand Canyon,
Or"—*sip, sip* of champagne—"the four stages
Of the Rodney King Riots."

He lifts a glass to his face,
Rivers of lines around his mouth,
The deltas of every piece of gossip he helped spread.

"Can't," he answers.
"My fingernails chip easily."

I tip back my drink,
And size up this artist through a light buzz—
He needs those fingernails,
Needs them to claw his way up.

BREAKDOWN ON A SMALL ROAD

The tire flat, Aladdin's smoky promise
Under the car's hood...I'm thirty
Miles from Goshen, a place
Nobody wants to stop.
Car, I whimper, why have you failed me?

A blackbird, hoodlum of the country sky,
Settles on the trunk and scolds me.
I throw a hatchet of hate at that hateful bird
And turn when I hear a bray:
A donkey on the other side of the wire.

Flies leap when I pet its nose.
I look into the eyes of this trusty beast
And view myself: ears large, teeth yellowish,
Flies a plague around my dirty face.
Will I climb its hide and ride off into the sunset?

The donkey pulls away and slowly moves to a bathtub
Set in the pasture, a greenish swill where the donkey drinks,
Sheep and clod-colored prairie mice drink.
And are those polliwogs flopping in mud,
Or turds coming alive?

After three days,
If a shadow appears, assume it's a blackbird.
If it's a trembling shadow, assume it's me, a thirsty apostle,
Parting the waters with greedy hands.

Fall wind through pine and oak,
And whistling across the teeth of purple-flowered thistle.
Our tracks are in the dust, our scent on the fence we straddle—
What mountain lion will sniff the air for our whereabouts?

I'm with a friend whose memory is like those tracks—
The angle of the sun first fills them with shadow.
Later, wind will climb down
From the trees and sweep them away.
"Leonard, it's not far," I say to my scholarly friend,
And I have in mind a table under an oak,
Near the archery course where Cupid is a rustic in overalls.

Leonard stops, grips my shoulder at the rusty squeak
Of a bird. "That's a…, that's a…"
His brow is plowed with lines, but he just can't remember.
My guess would be a sparrow, or a scolding jay,
Two birds I know besides the one on the Thanksgiving table.
He tightens his fist and squeaks, "My memory."
Some of it is with me, though. I recall Leonard
Lamenting the Speckled Eider, or was it the Snow Bunting?
How he hunkered under branches and held his breath.
A pair of binoculars rising to his face.

I creep, cat-quiet, when he says, "Go look there."
There is a tangle of brush. When I waddle into the undergrowth,
I find a clutch of sorrowful litter—a bottle cap, the cellophane
Of a cigarette pack, a buckled Pepsi can
And the Styrofoam clam shell of Chinese takeout.
I don't have the heart to tell him.
"The Speckled Eider," I whisper, "nah, a Snow Bunting!"

Who will believe me, the true novice and city dweller,
When I gush to my friend whose memory is gone,
Leonard, Leonard amigo, they're mating.

On a diet, I move the salt shaker like a chess piece,
And the pepper follows. Forget eggs,
Forget that steak wrapped in butcher paper,
And let's not dwell on the Freudian meaning
Of half-and-half cream.

(We get older. The cornucopia
Of spleen, kidney, and liver bruised,
Our joints stiff, our lives a glint in the rearview mirror.
The hair on your head just that—a hair.)

The red-nibbled radish is OK,
The glass of water with the milk ring on the bottom,
The apple, the pear, the orange quartered cleanly,
And a mob of grapes. I think,
My lunch is nothing but a still life!

But it's life. When I open the refrigerator,
I'm greeted by Mrs. Butterworth and her nemesis, Quaker Oats.
The beer looks beer-bellied—why didn't I see that earlier!
And the tortillas! I'm sure if you threw one
Onto the burner, Jesus' face would appear.

Wallace Stevens, poet and insurance salesman,
Once rolled up his pant legs and stood on a lapping shore.
From that tug of nature, he wrote three books,
So moved was he by the little act of slapping sand from his toes.

I have no shore, no insurance, no letter that begins, "My Dear Love."
In a park I could fall face first into autumn leaves
And rub my wounds until those leaves healed me.

Then I could go home, my mind big as a canvas.
My brushes are stiff, and the first figures just sticks,
But I can do a still life—the apple
And pear, the grapes in the biggest bowl.
In the background, the salt and pepper shakers, their red tops—
My yearning, critics would say, to roughhouse with a bloody steak?

BOOKS BY GARY SOTO

One Kind of Faith

Amnesia in a Republican County

Poetry Lover

The Effects of Knut Hamsun on a Fresno Boy

Jessie De La Cruz: A Profile of a United Farm Worker

A Natural Man

Nickel and Dime

Junior College

Buried Onions

New and Selected Poems

Jesse

Pieces of the Heart

Home Course in Religion

Who Will Know Us?

A Summer Life

California Childhood

Black Hair

Living Up the Street

Lesser Evils

Small Faces

Where Sparrows Work Hard

The Tale of Sunlight

The Elements of San Joaquin

Jay Blakesberg

GARY SOTO is a poet, playwright, essayist, and author of several
children's books. Widely anthologized, he is a frequent contributor
to such magazines as the *Threepenny Review, Michigan Quarterly
Review, Crazy Horse*, and *Poetry*, which has honored him with both
the Bess Hokin and Levinson Prizes. He has received the Discovery/
The Nation Award, as well as the Andrew Carnegie Medal for
Excellence in Children's Video, the Literature Award from the
Hispanic Heritage Foundation, and an American Book Award from
the Before Columbus Foundation. He has also received fellowships
from the John Simon Guggenheim Memorial Foundation, the
National Endowment for the Arts, and the California Arts Council.
A National Book Award finalist for *New and Selected Poems*
(Chronicle Books), Gary Soto divides his time between Berkeley and
his hometown of Fresno.